We hope you enjoy this book as much as we do!

GOOD NIGHT NIGHT-MARES

Good Night Nightmares
First published in 2012 in Spain
by Editorial Casals, S.A
Text © 2012 Elisenda Roca
Illustrations © 2012 Cristina Losantos
English Translation © 2014 Quirky Kid

ISBN: 978-0-9806743-7-8

Good Night Nightmares
Published in Australia in
2014 by Quirky Kid
ABN 38 688 198 104,
PO Box 598, Woollahra
NSW 2025, Australia

A Quirky Kid Production.
Visit www.quirkykid.com.au for a catalogue.

The National Library of Australia
Cataloguing-in Publication.
Dewey Number: 863.7

© 2014 Copyright Quirky Kid.
All rights reserved. No Part of this
publication may be used or reproduced,
stored in a retrieval system, or transmitted
in any form or by any means (electronic,
mechanical, photocopying, recording,
or otherwise) without the prior written
permission of the publisher.

ELISENDA ROCA
CRISTINA LOSANTOS
Translation By:
BARBARA GONZALEZ
TOM VECK

A story to ward off night time fears.

J osh was quite the happy lad,
  kind, polite and rarely bad.
He never lied and loved his school,
he shared his toys with one and all.

He loved to eat and clean his plate
(except for spinach which he hates).
His mum, she said, "Don't grumble and moan,
you'll like it better as you grow."

In the day come rain or shine,
Josh was cheerful, happy and fine.
But as the daytime turned to black,
his nervous worries all came back.

"What's the matter, love?" said Mum.
"Are you worried night has come?"
"Perhaps you'd like some milk and honey?"
But Josh couldn't think about his tummy.

After a cuddle, Dad tucked him into bed,
"Lights out now, there's nothing to dread."
"But it's way too dark!" poor Josh, he cried,
for now he had nowhere to hide.

All alone and in the dark
Josh stiffened at the sight.
A shadow man behind the door
leapt out! - oh what a fright!

Josh screamed a mighty piercing scream,
his ma and da arrived.
The light came on, Ma hugged him tight,
there'd been no need to hide.

They left him with his teddy bear
to comfort and to soothe him.
But just as Josh imagined,
another beast came looming.

A wicked, warty witch flew by
and a giant wanting dinner.
Plus goblins, ghosts and skeletons
and a goggle-eyed web spinner!

And when he thought he couldn't stand
another ghoulish figure,
from out behind the bedroom door
another came - but bigger!

"Phew!" said Josh, "thank goodness,
I'm so glad that it's you, Nan.
I've been so scared and worried
ever since this night began."

"Oh poor young Josh, what is it?
Whatever is the matter?"
Josh said, "The shadows in my room
were growing uglier and fatter!"

"These nasty creatures can't they see?
The sign is clear as day.
Scary things are not allowed -
NIGHTMARES GO AWAY"

"Your imagination is great and wild,
a tricky thing for every child.
So let's go out and play a game,
the dark will never be the same."

Out of the room and into the hall,
"Watch out there, don't trip or fall!
Switch off the light and stay alert,
I know you won't get hurt."

"Let's use our hands instead of our eyes,
and it may come as some surprise,
that nothing which we touch out here
will give us any cause to fear."

Tightly gripping his granny's hand,
Josh tiptoed bravely as they'd planned.
When something scraped across his head,
"EEK! A yucky spider's web!"

Courageously he looked to see,
"What is this horrid thing on me?"
Relieved and glad he laughed because
a dressing gown is all it was!

"The dragon's just a quilt," he said,
"and the robot with the scary head,
is just a silly cardboard box.
And that one's just a cuckoo clock!"

"The darkness isn't all that bad,
I can't believe it made me sad.
But look two more!" with dread, he said,
"No wait, that's Mum and Dad instead!"

"What a surprise, let's play again!"
Josh loved the brand new night time game.
"Turn out the lights and let's explore,
I love this game, let's play some more!"

So with a smile from ear to ear
Josh went to bed without a fear.
For all his fears were only thoughts,
no shadow beasts of any sort.

So if your mind plays tricks on you,
now you know what you can do.
Go face your fears and play the game,
night time will never be the same!

QuirkyKid®

Other Titles By Quirky Kid

The Likes of You{th}
Just Like When
How to Be a Friend
Face It Cards
Tell Me a Story Cards
Tickets - A tool to tame behaviour
Power Up - A performance psychology program

All Titles In This Series

Good Night Nightmares
It's Mine!
Hi! Thanks! Bye!
The Tale of The Three Little Grubs

More About Quirky Kid

The Quirky Kid Clinic is a unique place for children aged 2-18 years. We work from the Child's perspective and help families find their own solutions. We offer counselling and therapy, assessments, practical workshops as well as developing and publishing therapeutic resources.

For more information about our services, products and programs visit **www.QuirkyKid.com.au**.

Quirky Kid is a registered Trademark.